# Midnight Muse in a Convenience store

Daniel McTaggart

Edited by Shaw Israel Izikson

Copyright © 2018 Venetian Spider Press
and Daniel McTaggart

All rights reserved.

ISBN: 1-7326794-4-3
ISBN-13: 978-1-7326794-4-3

# Midnight Muse in a Convenience Store

For my crew of characters at the convenience store, some of whom have since passed -

Alicia, Harvey, Tom, Jim, Craig, Fireball, Clipper, Toad, Woody, Sam, and more.

You are all the heart of my time there.

# Midnight Muse in a Convenience Store

# Daniel McTaggart

## Contents

Window ............................................................................. 2
falling ................................................................................ 3
Moon Dances, Midnight Leads ........................................ 4
As If They Breathe ........................................................... 5
Matrimony ........................................................................ 6
Night of Numbers ............................................................ 7
Probe ................................................................................ 8
Wedding Night ................................................................. 9
Out of Reach .................................................................. 10
Avenue ........................................................................... 11
Crescendo ....................................................................... 12
Shameless Sky ............................................................... 13
Midnight Shift ................................................................ 14
Backyard Spider ............................................................. 15
Down Beat ..................................................................... 16
Sleepless Bird ................................................................. 17
Casino Weather .............................................................. 18
Bittersweet Thunder ....................................................... 19
Fog With Full Stomach .................................................. 20
Dianaluna ....................................................................... 21
Scavenging ..................................................................... 22
Monongahela Horizon ................................................... 23
Fogswim ........................................................................ 24
Morning's Pale Breath ................................................... 25

## Midnight Muse in a Convenience Store

Cobblestone Hill ................................................................... 26
Not So Dear .......................................................................... 27
Arrow Heading ..................................................................... 28
Stumpjumper ........................................................................ 29
Rhythms ............................................................................... 30
Paper and Pencil ................................................................... 31
Funeral Parlors ..................................................................... 32
Unborn .................................................................................. 33
Patience Unbidden ............................................................... 34
Windy ................................................................................... 35
A Place to Play .................................................................... 36
I Was Not Here .................................................................... 37
Bones of Autumn ................................................................. 38
Interlude on the Pennsylvania Turnpike: 1975 ................... 39
Still Soldiers ........................................................................ 40
Gopher Hunt ........................................................................ 41
Voice of Winter ................................................................... 42
On Going to Poetry Readings ............................................. 43
Quiet Notes ......................................................................... 44
Graveyard ............................................................................ 45
Salt Lick Moon ................................................................... 46
Electric Tang ....................................................................... 47
Private Comedy ................................................................... 48
The Breath That Gods Blow ............................................... 49
Woman Wears Pants for the First Time ............................. 50

## Daniel McTaggart

She's Gotta Go ................................................................51
Injured Swan ..................................................................52
Midnight Muse in a Convenience Store......................53
Turtle Girl .......................................................................54
Convenience Store Coquette.........................................55
Blue Law.........................................................................56
Midnight Ripple .............................................................57
Well-dressed Black Woman Asking for Hotel Directions
..........................................................................................58
Moon Baked....................................................................59
Crutches ..........................................................................60
A Tale From Behind the Register .................................61
Moth.................................................................................62
Pledges ............................................................................63
Clearing...........................................................................64
On Today's Episode .......................................................65
Sprucing Up ....................................................................66
Dumb Finger ...................................................................67
Deputy Sam.....................................................................68
Rodney Dangerous..........................................................69
Cure for a Drunk Girlfriend ..........................................70
Quick Whispers...............................................................71
ABOUT THE AUTHOR ................................................72

Midnight Muse in a Convenience Store

# Midnight Muse in a Convenience Store

Daniel McTaggart

Window

I am a window
Look through me

Past sunlit strands of
Dust hanging in air
Clinging to panes

Clouds are glazed
Pink and orange bleeding
Shades of midnight

Stand close and watch
Ancient storms
Fierce and wonderful

Trees and houses melt
Porch lights swirl and streak
Rippling at your touch

I am your window
See through me

## Midnight Muse in a Convenience Store

falling

thes
now(i
sth
etim
efo
rlo
ve)f
all
s

### Daniel McTaggart

## Moon Dances, Midnight Leads

moon dangles on a spider's web
a dewdrop bathed in azure

clouds capture the glow
swaying like evening gowns to
the whims of midnight waltzing

moon is such a delicate partner
never missing a limber step

dancing on velvet floors
toward ballroom's end
fading in the morning star

# Midnight Muse in a Convenience Store

## As If They Breathe

I feel lucky to see stars
To see them blink
As if they breathe

I wonder if they float
Or are they pinpricks
In a velvet tarp

City lights on horizons
Give off cold sparkles
Mimicking warm flickers

I watch stars as if
They breathe with me
And think of missing family

## Daniel McTaggart

### Matrimony

cars roaming at night
carry whispers
vanishing as they pass

dragging silence in their wake
ethereal cans tied
to invisible strings

elemental couples racing
away to honeymoons
from secret marriages

# Midnight Muse in a Convenience Store

## Night of Numbers

one full moon lingers high
its halo bore through clouds

two stars glimmer meekly
subdued by the brutal glow

three cars dash by, dopplered
laughter escaping windows

four leaves break off their perch
clattering together in soft breezes

five steps I take from lights
standing unfettered under stars

draped in their dark
dappled cloak breathing

Daniel McTaggart

Probe

The high moon glazes the land blue
Heavy mist snakes low
Around moss-covered maples

Coarse air is caressed by
Chirps of lonely crickets
Tall grasses twitching

If night could move
This would be the merest
Brush of a fingertip

# Midnight Muse in a Convenience Store

## Wedding Night

Clouds are laundry at
The mercy of evening breeze

Stars glimmer like eyes
Under a half-moon

A thin blanket slides
Off a mattress

Chains of autumn leaves drag
A marriage has taken place

The moon and wind are
Tonight's bride and groom

We have been witnesses as all
The stars have laid in waiting

Daniel McTaggart

## Out of Reach

the full moon can
not fight city lights

its glow bleeds slow
ly into candlewick clouds

ethereal frays swirl
ing around like the hun

gry tongue of a moth
too numb from risk

the full moon widens
with child's won

der at wanting to
touch any pret

ty thing that passes

## Midnight Muse in a Convenience Store

Avenue

at night
raindrops spatter
on glass panes of street lamps
scattering their glow to the path
below

Daniel McTaggart

Crescendo

pianissimo fog rides coattails
of concerto rain

descending sleek crests
of rhythmic drops

staccato pit-a-pats fading
on drum tight pavement

## Midnight Muse in a Convenience Store

Shameless Sky

tattered
clouds float across
the full moon like veils tossed
aside by a promiscuous
dancer

Daniel McTaggart

Midnight Shift

There is no noise at true midnight
There is no breakwater against
Expansion of the senses

Nothing to stop us seeing sounds
Darkness tells us trees
Do night fight the wind

To tips of fingers
Strumming ancient instruments
Each tree is a singular tune

There is something more
To the flutter of leaves
A message being passes

A language discerned only
By delicate attentions
Without clumsy tongues

So we may read a branch to say
That was no bob in the wind
That was a word

# Midnight Muse in a Convenience Store

Backyard Spider

precarious
needlepoint stride

sitting still, smooth
suspended in wind

draped in lace
spun from morning dew

serene like death
till company comes

Daniel McTaggart

Down Beat

nothing but wind
in my ears at 4 am
outside the store

a flag rope taps
against a steel pole
waiting for partners

dawn will arrive
on the down beat
of a midnight waltz

# Midnight Muse in a Convenience Store

Sleepless Bird

At 3:30 am soft rain
Suffused with acrid
Odor of wet pavement

A sleepless bird chirps
In the void, forgetting
Politics of the clock

Desperate lovers roaming
Clinging in midnight miasma
The plasma of predawn

Other birds may preen
And prance in the sun
It's not their territory

## Daniel McTaggart

### Casino Weather

thunderclaps roll
around corrugated clouds

electric spheres
on a roulette wheel

where lightning strikes
nobody knows

## Midnight Muse in a Convenience Store

Bittersweet Thunder

As humidity rises, shadowy
Surfaces reflect flickering

Licorice and twisty twines cast
Down from chocolate clouds

The darker they become the more
Bittersweet their thunder,

Rage falling in powdered smatters
The ground laying sweet and still

Daniel McTaggart

Fog With Full Stomach

Mist has eaten most of midnight
Laying leaden by a large meal

Below the level of morning's shelf
Like a sleepless snake it shifts

From digestion of its activities
Belching sounds of an idle town

Limping off pace with the rising sun
Before the next night is served

## Midnight Muse in a Convenience Store

Dianaluna

the tilt of her expression
agape, astonished

her face tarnished yellow by soot
shreds obscuring her glow

her surprise should be no wonder
since only she may see

the truth behind her light

Daniel McTaggart

## Scavenging

before 6 am, city lights are
pearls in a black bed

like the moon they lose
pace with the approach of dawn

cars frenzy with piercing eyes
scavenging for the smoothest glows

even at daybreak these cars
still roam with feelers

# Midnight Muse in a Convenience Store

## Monongahela Horizon

sunrise
slips like red wine
seeping through cloudy cracks
stars depart like champagne bubbles
rising

# Daniel McTaggart

## Fogswim

wading through morning
invisible hills howl in my ears

echoes swallowed by distance
draw fetal contractions in the fog

it swirls like sand
at my fingers, at my arms

fanning slowly so I may watch
dancing until sun burns it away

# Midnight Muse in a Convenience Store

## Morning's Pale Breath

midnight steals smoke
from dormant mountaintops

leaves twitch as morning's pale
breath shuttles between branches

cars pass as dual cones
plowing through the soup

resonating and rising like
the breath of all living things

Daniel McTaggart

Cobblestone Hill

Along Route 19 south
Past the point of Jones' Rain
Lies a rocky mound
Shaped something like a wall

Or perhaps a barrier, but for what
Remains a mystery
Maybe shelter for midday lovers
A rampart for soldiers dodging fire

Whatever these stones could say
Is muted by a blanket of snow
Meaning for every battle fought over it
The visitors are lost to time

# Midnight Muse in a Convenience Store

Not So Dear

I would rather all my money earned
Was plucked from out my pocket
Than one line from poem purloined
From my deepest mental socket

My hardest won collectibles
Are not so dear to me
That I would give my soul to sharks
Who frenzy in the sea

To scribe my soul is such a gift
That I give unto myself
I could never fritter it away
So it stays upon the shelf

# Daniel McTaggart

## Arrow Heading

Dad and I would hunt
Arrowheads on barren farmland

Turning over sun-cracked
Soil with gnarled canes

Cicadas cackling under windless
Skies in needle prick heat

History teaches us Indians
Peppered these lands with skirmishes

Arrowheads plucked from parched
Pavement smoothed and rippled

As though just flung from ancient
Bows targeting my cradled hands

# Midnight Muse in a Convenience Store

Stumpjumper

Here come a lawman
Pokin' round my still

Don' have no plan
Jus' goin' where he will

But he won't catch me
I'm hidin' behind a tree

I try to sneak away
Snappin' twigs under my boot

That lawman gonna work hard today
Jumpin' stumps in hot pursuit

But he won't catch me
'Cause Lord I'm runnin' free

Daniel McTaggart

Rhythms

If I read you a poem
Would you hear its rhythms?

If you were deaf
What part of you would listen?
What part of you would not hear?

If you would hear my rhythms
Would you see them as they fly?
What would feather their wings?

Would it be fog or lace of
Something we have never named?

How would you interpret them?
In the way poets do?
Or would you simply understand?

Perhaps I write because I understand
Or because I don't

Perhaps I've been reading
Answers to all my secrets
And you heard something else

# Midnight Muse in a Convenience Store

Paper and Pencil

Women are like paper
Written upon, still
Speaking between the lines

Illegible lovers turn them like pages
But there are no pictures

Men are like pencils
Stiff, full of lead, and sharp
Until they write on virgin surfaces

Light and lengthy strokes
Do not dull their edge too quickly

Sometimes the pencil snaps
From pressing to hard
Thick marks erase not so easily

Sometimes paper cuts
If creased too closely

Apart from each other
Their functions are incomplete
Together they scuff each other blunt

Perhaps if correspondence is not too trite
Paper and pencil should learn how to write

Daniel McTaggart

## Funeral Parlors

I would see
People cry who
Never cried before
At least
Not in front of me

I would sit
In the front row
Watching them pass by in tears
They were
So beautiful to me

I would think
About how lovely
They all looked at
That moment
Of slow precious time

I would know
That sometimes
Such grace is not
Always brought
Out in happier ways

## Midnight Muse in a Convenience Store

Unborn

Night is
An eye

The moon
A glimmer of a child

See the face of what
He or she may become

Find the same
Light in your face

If you would
Be blessed

Daniel McTaggart

Patience Unbidden

Winds gust breathlessly
Trees sway and slump with
The weight of a tired back

Slowly rocking in tandem
She stares with listless
Eyes through a rusted screen

Clouds color the ground
As raindrops pool in craters
Of speckled sidewalk

She cradles her legs under
A baggy sweater, her long hair
A lazy snake on her bare shoulder

A bluebird crouches on a bobbing
Branch, with the same gaze
Waiting for love that will never come

# Midnight Muse in a Convenience Store

*Windy*

In younger days, Windy bellowed
From all the way out in centerfield.
Batters must have fathomed no other
Reason for a strong summer breeze.

Later a little girl says "Smile, Daddy,"
While he shovels manure.
He casts a toothy grin
Just as the camera clicks.

Still later, playing Wiffle Ball,
A little boy asks grandpa for the bat.
"No," says grandpa.
"I'm going to swing all night."

One must have thought
That strong summer breeze came
From a laugh he hadn't done
Since he was twenty-one.

And perhaps, behind those sharp
Steely squinting eyes,
Behind the wide and wily grin,
He'd been swinging ever since.

Daniel McTaggart

A Place to Play

I think our grandparents' farm would be
A perfect place to play,
Running through roofless fields,
Laughing at cows swatting flies,
Chasing rabbits through rows of corn.

I think that place would keep us from
The fear of scraping out knees,
But we are at play here.
And what is play but a license for scabby knees.

Such a place gets smaller as we get bigger.
As we grow, we tend to follow serious
Paths sometimes mistaken for maturity.
And what is maturity but a license
For knowing when to play.

We all need a place to play.
To dash down grassy slopes
Fast enough to feel wind
Wrapping around our ears.

So when we reach the top of another hill
We catch our breath, and then
We start running again,
A race that never ends.

# Midnight Muse in a Convenience Store

## I Was Not Here

Walter wrote his name
Upon a big rock
It said he was here, yet
He was nowhere

The next day I came back
And saw Bill was here with Martha
They and Walter were
Here but not there

With every trip back
More people were here
So many days, so many people
Here and not here

I decided to write my name
So they all would know
That I was here
Though I wasn't there

The next day I came back
To see if I was here
They wrote to me and said
I was not here

So there I was

## Daniel McTaggart

### Bones of Autumn

Winter stretches beneath autumn covers
Colored quilts recede further

Revealing sugared hills under brittle dawn
Vibrance erodes into ash

Crumbling at the kindle of pallid sun
The bare bones of autumn gather

A silver skin flying away
On every whispered wind

## Midnight Muse in a Convenience Store

Interlude on the Pennsylvania Turnpike: 1975

By the roadside
a blue car's front
end was crumpled

A blonde woman slumped
in the passenger seat
peacefully

In our front seat
an old man in a blanket
sits moaning

Blood-laced over his mottled, bald head
A moustached stranger sits with him
He asks my brother and I about school

Mom and dad are outside
hovering around the wreckage
Mom presses the woman's temple

A small creek
carries away
leaking gasoline

The stranger asks how old we are
I let my brother speak
My attention is held by blood

and the old man
glistening as he rattles

## Daniel McTaggart

### Still Soldiers
*for Harvey, a veteran and friend*

These men are still soldiers
Bullets still scream through air
Choppers still fan tall blades of grass

They walk streets in your town
Some shuffling in dirty fatigues
Wiping spit from their brow

You are why they went to war
You are why they walked in gore
You who look their way no more

You can't know the warm splash of blood on your face
You can't see your friends falling and shattered
You can't feel guts spilling into your hands

They fought so you wouldn't have to know
They still fight
And you still don't know

# Midnight Muse in a Convenience Store

## Gopher Hunt

A farmer's son with a wicked pun
Is whistling wise with cocksure fun
He's shooting gophers with a gun
While walking in the morning sun

His boots do on the cut hay crackle
As distant crows fling echoed cackle
Gopher blood spurts out like spackle
But his wee job is hardly done

He brushes gun smoke off his shirt
One gopher only sprawls the dirt
With Death his gaping maw does flirt
A spider's web is barely spun

He strides along to thicker patches
Suffering more nicks and scratches
Looking for a hole that matches
Where a hunted mole would run

He shoots and sings till evening sets
Each pellet flies with no regrets
Their exits chased by gushing jets
That sparkle in the sinking sun

Daniel McTaggart

Voice of Winter

When weather changes
Winds wear swift shoes

Clouds are tarnished by dust
Kicked up by runners' treads

What had been sweet and temperate
Is now flavored with sharp tang

With the sun masked, turning
Leaves burn with dull flame

Foretelling Winter's grip
Before the eyes of Autumn close

# Midnight Muse in a Convenience Store

## On Going to Poetry Readings

Whenever I went to a poetry reading
I watched the author gaze

Upon the gathered crowd, thinking
How impressed he must be

To see us all here
Just to listen to him

But no

He knew we were all waiting
To hear him slip on a metaphor

To see him stare up
With word on his face

## Daniel McTaggart

### Quiet Notes

lights on, lights on
lights on above me

dreaming all my past illusions
under a shower of dust
colored reflections fall
sheeting down a window pane

lights on, lights on
lights on around me

propping my feet crossed on the table
tapping on air to elemental music
quiet notes such as
the touch of dust upon the floor

## Midnight Muse in a Convenience Store

Graveyard

night shift
thick with dark calm
gas pumps stand like tombstones
drivers pay for epitaphs with
credit

## Daniel McTaggart

### Salt Lick Moon

As I drive, night resonates
Distended echoes of my home

Full moon is freakishly agape
Horrified by the sight of

A life I left far behind
She was supposed to be a partner

On this journey to new lands
Instead she looks back

Upon the ashes of Gomorrah
Unable to cast eyes aside

For penance she hangs
Pilloried in midnight skies

A ball of salt licked by stars
Her face reflecting

The glow of a life she loved
Lost through a selfish act

## Midnight Muse in a Convenience Store

Electric Tang

aimless breezes dart across
dark lanes while lights
hum with electric tang

strolling lovers bathe in tart glow
scuffing sandaled feet
along littered curves

at some point amidst the buzzing
a low chuckle
muffled in the darkness

Daniel McTaggart

Private Comedy

They come in after dark
Strolling the aisles
Studying labels and brand names

A man searches for a type of gum
Twitching like a chipmunk
Deciding whether to store a nut

A woman shuffles to a rack
Trying every pair of sunglasses
Primping with hair up and down

A college girl pulls up to a pump
She squeegees every fixture clean
Leaving with a satisfied nod

None of them realize what they are
Unintentional actors on stage
Stopping between engagements

All performing private scenes
Of accidental amusement
We rarely find otherwise

## Midnight Muse in a Convenience Store

### The Breath That Gods Blow

Friday nights bring steady streams of
Intoxicated women vending
False confidence of immature men

Sampling vapors of feminine wares
Inhaling with feral pride
Women who are petty and jealous

As ancient deities clawing each other
They are motes of dust riding
The current of enticing whims

Weekends carry electric thrills
For people coming like
From the lungs of a god

Be still and you may sense
A yawning
A mouthing of an ice cream cone

Wait and chirp as a legless cricket
Basking in long slow
Sighs of a woman's walk

Daniel McTaggart

Woman Wears Pants for the First Time

Words cannot ever express
Why she does not wear a dress
So the pants will take a stand
Let the hem talk to the hand

# Midnight Muse in a Convenience Store

## She's Gotta Go

Sporting a handkerchief top
Painted on jeans

Hips jerking like a munchkin's
From the lollipop guild

She places a hand for balance
On her girlfriend's shoulder

Who rolls her eyes
Clamping the dancing girl's hand

Pulling her toward the bathroom
In the shape of a question

## Daniel McTaggart

Injured Swan

She gazes at her reflection
In the lake, garbled,
Warped by passing ripples

Feathers rest unevenly at her side
So she starves herself
To subdue her plumage

Strength and confidence wane
With every look
In her own twisted mirror

## Midnight Muse in a Convenience Store

She saunters through the door
Accompanied by a breath of smoke
Her summer dress swaying
To the whims of her hips
And the tug of her breasts

Slowly she strides the aisles
Skidding her sandaled feet
As she pauses by the milk
Her head lolls over her shoulder
Like a lazy flower

She opens the cooler door
Slender painted fingers reach up
Threading long auburn hair
Falling in a gossamer fan
Across her small back

After taking a gallon of milk
She briskly rubs a tanned tender calf
Brushing away a sharp chill to no avail
It slithers up along her limber frame
Demanding a sultry shiver

She asks for the time
Her voice a feathery husk
Her smile a slim smirk
Her oval eyes like echoes
Flooding with green

## Daniel McTaggart

### Turtle Girl

she fronts
her carapace
like a wise sea turtle
fending off raging predators
and men

# Midnight Muse in a Convenience Store

## Convenience Store Coquette

alabaster skin
under a flimsy black smock

breasts surge outward
torpedoes cleaving air

her masculine girlfriend
as she walks out the door

grabs a handful of ass

Daniel McTaggart

Blue Law

He came in one
Minute after two
Went to the cooler for
A 12-pack of brew

He said to me
I'm buying the beer
Look at my watch
One minute left here

I said I have one minute more
It's one minute too late
And his yellow teeth
Started to grate

I said if you want the beer
You can buy it
Pay my fine sit in jail for me
Go ahead try it

## Midnight Muse in a Convenience Store

Midnight Ripple

When bars have served last call
Pretty girls stumble through doors

I sit where they don't expect
I like the small hop they make

Best when accompanied by
A sharp squeal of surprise

It breaks against me
A tide threading my toes

# Daniel McTaggart

## Well-dressed Black Woman Asking for Hotel Directions

she wants lettuce on both
sides of her sandwich

forgetting

it does not spread
easily as mayonnaise

but then
it's only 3 am

## Midnight Muse in a Convenience Store

### Moon Baked

At four o'clock in the morning country
Music rides feathered curls of
Smoke suspended in phosphorescent air
Beneath pockmarked plaster ceilings

Waitresses fan smoke away
With torn and faded menus
Corners worn thin by
Palms of late night travelers

A man with glasses sits in a booth
Chuckling over the latest issue of Mad
Waiting on his wife driving her friend home
He didn't want to share the car with him

The hostess pauses by her reflection
Fluffing her thinning auburn hair
Haranguing the hairy cook over
An order of runny scrambled eggs

She freshens your coffee
You stare out toward
The moon-baked highway
It's time to hit the road again

## Daniel McTaggart

Crutches

Walking in before dawn
Black hair fastened over his eyes
By a damp red ball cap

He's been smoking for nine years
He's been drinking for twenty

He carries a crutch by his side
He has no limp

# Midnight Muse in a Convenience Store

## A Tale From Behind the Register

Weathery nights pass into silent mornings
Limping old men stroll in for coffee
Smiling and waving
Greeting their fellow liars

They sip and they blather
About hunting and retirement
Sniping each other over
Bad hair and no hair

Coffee wanes and they leave to tell
The same lies somewhere else
Disheveled women shuffle inside
Food Stamps fanned like full houses

Their blank stares speak of
Bruises surrounding their faces
Gathering bags they walk outside
Wordlessly with skeletal grace

Pausing in mid-stride
Looking over bony shoulders
To make contact with anyone
Then turn and go unnoticed

Sunlight cycles down to dusk
Cars pass by immaterial
Just two tandem lights
Racing for young love

# Daniel McTaggart

## Moth

Around two or three in the morning
The canopy lights may as well be moons
The gas pumps branchless, unable to
Disseminate the glow, making it a pure
Source for creatures tired of occasional slips

I thought it was a leaf fallen from
Some grand old maple in a
Nearby yard shared by trailers
Wide and yellow as befits the start
Of my favorite season of bodily chill
And warm sweet beverages to swill
While colors loop out like pulled threads

But its wings were undessicated by cold
Segments of its body pulsed in waiting
No other customers intruded
As the hours pressed in layers
Thinner than heather, cooler than
Ivy hugging a shaded wall, drying up at
The merest brush of rising sun, that's how
Easily a mystery can escape between glances

# Midnight Muse in a Convenience Store

## Pledges

A local sorority brought prospective
Members in the store one afternoon
My boss said it was something
They did every year
Though I only saw it happen once

Some girls were made to run
Laps around the gas pumps
In the manner of fires figure eighting above
Corpses bloating on littered roadsides
They ran with elbows flapping in
Sorry attempts to catch updrafts

Other girls were brought in the store
Blindfolded, arms stretching
Out over shelves of chips, cookies,
And slick magazines, and they
Had to guess the nature of all they touched
I came up to one girl's ear and told her
They were sending her home with me

## Daniel McTaggart

### Clearing

I was allowed to come to work
In old dirty clothes one sunny day
The hill behind the store needed
Clearing of briars, ivy leaves, and shrubs

And even though it was cool outside
I stood inside the cooler on my breaks
Drinking free Kool-Aid behind the
Racks of soda, beer, and milk

Bathed in cold green aura of
Mountain Dew, I watched while
Customers studied expiration dates
And even then preferring to drink diet

I never inferred a ratio of calories to guilt
I saw thirst as replacing what
I lost on that hill pulling out
Vines long buried in old showers of

Cigarette butts and cookie wrappers
Torn open by corroded teeth
Covering the hill like abandoned parachutes
And I spent my entire shift cutting strings

# Midnight Muse in a Convenience Store

On Today's Episode

As I threw out the trash, two
Women were smoking behind
The dumpster

Just standing and puffing
They were sisters and they were waiting

One girl arrived to work a bit late
Dropped off by her boyfriend
Which is when his wife and
Sister-in-law charged across the lot

Cigarettes and curse words clenched
Outpacing their smoke
Threading their flying copper wire hair

Pouncing and pummeling on him while
She ran back to the office
Locking the door tight while he
Held onto his kicking-punching wife

The sister-in-law declared that woman
Couldn't stay back there forever
That she couldn't stay on this property
Forever, but she was out of breath
And smoke was standing outside the door

Daniel McTaggart

Sprucing Up

A girl came in one night and she
Walked slowly through the aisles

College girl, I thought, stopping by
For a few things she didn't know
She needed

I approved a couple of cars by the pumps
Then I heard strange hissing
Turning to see the girl placing
Spray deodorant on the shelf as she
Went toward the cooler doors

Just testing the scent, perhaps seeing if
She wouldn't mind smelling like that

So I began counting tobacco sales when
She circled around again to give
Her hair a spritz or two using
Shiny shelf trim as a trick mirror
For threading her curls out

She got Dew and gum and
She smelled damn good

# Midnight Muse in a Convenience Store

## Dumb Finger

Jim came for coffee every morning
Jeans dusty from mixing concrete
That had to be poured early in the day

So why not have a cup or two while it sets
What else is a retired fireman to do

He was saying how he lifted something
Too heavy and felt a snap
A warm chill going up his arm
Now he couldn't move his forefinger at all

To demonstrate, he strummed on it
And it went back like a banjo string

Locked in permanent point, his other
Hand was unburdened of directional use
As lines disappeared, it became
A tube used only for balance when

Holding coffee cups and steering wheels
He also used it to stress the correctness
Of any argument he'd otherwise lose

Daniel McTaggart

Deputy Sam

Not every night, but usually when the moon
Was new he'd show up to shoot
The bull in memory of all the arguments
He used to shoot down, the hammer
Always cocked behind his .45 caliber face

But Sam was never mean, his body was
The rudder for an easy smile
He swayed up to the register
With a beer and a plastic cup

Nodding toward darkness just beyond
The double doors twitching from a
Quick breath, I rang him up

He'd already poured when I met him
Out on the back deck, and it was
Too dark for anything else with
Eyes and bad hearing

To witness him taking a sip
Even I only saw a glint off his glasses
And a sparkle from his ring whenever
It was raised in dedication to stolen time

## Midnight Muse in a Convenience Store

Rodney Dangerous

Rodney liked to hug pretty girls
Approaching them his favorite
Way, from behind

He liked surprise on their faces
As they turned to see a guy who
Pretended he couldn't speak

The pity they felt overwhelmed any
Sense of caution about a strange
Dumpy Coke bottle glasses dude

He was harmless sitting by windows
Penning love letters to Pamela Anderson
Checking favorite street corners on city maps

The blonder the girl, the braver
He became until I told him to stop
Then he swiped all the pennies

In the manner of children
Reaching for M&M's or
The biggest strawberries

I still see him pausing on littered roadsides
Licking chocolate or vanilla pity cones
His pockets bursting with ones

Daniel McTaggart

## Cure for a Drunk Girlfriend

Thursdays were ladies' nights downtown
So their boyfriends came in Friday
Mornings asking for something
Really anything with bread

And in West Virginia
That meant pepperoni rolls

Those original coal miners' lunches
Easy to bake, easy to take down
Deep in the mines holding up
Hunger as they held up our state

And on Fridays guys fed girlfriends
Something to hold up their bodies

Otherwise they slide off to one side
Limp as children tipping over hammocks
Faces slumping on windows stretching
Like silly putty Sunday funnies

# Midnight Muse in a Convenience Store

## Quick Whispers

We had two booths in the store
Painted in equal coats of setting sun
Highlighting arcs of dust missed
By short rags, and a few lone crumbs
Casting needlepoint shadows

Even from the register I saw flies
Turned on their backs, legs twiddling
Akimbo, too dumb to find
The door they flew through

It's more of a painting when a guy sits
Down for a cup of black coffee
Steam rolling over a Styrofoam brim

He's looking out the window seeming
Happier with every car passing by
Fading in the clatter of
Spare change sorted on the counter

Daniel McTaggart

ABOUT THE POET

Daniel McTaggart, the West Virginia Beat Poet Laureate from 2017 - 2019, has had his poetry published in *Amomancies*, *Kestrel*, and *Backbone Mountain Review*. He has also appeared in a recent volume of *Bards Against Hunger* and *BEAT-itude*, and edited *Stranger to Blue Water*, all from Local Gems Poetry Press. He edited *Diner Stories: Off the Menu* from Mountain State Press, appeared in *the best of amomancies* from Venetian Spider Press, and self-published *Diner Poems* among other chapbooks.

He lives in Morgantown, West Virginia, and believes it's not a diner unless coffee is in the air.

www.ingramcontent.com/pod-product-compliance
Lightning Source LLC
Chambersburg PA
CBHW071356160426
42811CB00112B/2334/J